Title Information:	
Date:	
Logbook #:	
Continued from Logbook #:	
Name:	
Title:	
Address:	
City & State:	
Email address:	
Telephone #:	
Date Logbook Started	
Date Logbook Ended	
Signature	

Notes:-

TABLE OF CONTENTS

DATE	SUBJECT	PAGE#

TABLE OF CONTENTS

DATE	SUBJECT	PAGE#

TABLE OF CONTENTS

DATE	SUBJECT	PAGE#

	Date: ___/___/___	Page # 2
		Book #

	Date: ___/___/___	Page # 4
		Book #

	Date: ___/___/___	Page # 5
		Book #

	Date:	Page # 6
_____	___/___/___	Book #

	Date:	Page # 7
	___/___/___	Book #

	Date:	Page # 10
	___/___/___	Book #

	Date: ___/___/___	Page # 17
		Book #

Date: ___/___/___

Date: ___/___/___

Book #

Quick

Quick

	Date: ___/___/___	Page # 26
		Book #

	Date:	Page # 28
	___/___/___	Book #

Date:

___/___/___

	Date:	Page # 42
	___/___/____	Book #

	Date:	Page # 56
	___/___/___	Book #

	Date:	Page # 62
	___/___/___	Book #

	Date: ___/___/___	Page # 74
		Book #

	Date: ___/___/___	Page # 83
		Book #

	Date: ___/___/___	Page # 86
		Book #

Date: ___/___/___

Page # 100

Book #

	Date: ___/___/___	Page # 105
		Book #